Medea and Other Poems of the Anthropocene

Medea and Other Poems of the Anthropocene

Poetry by

Dawid Juraszek

Cover design by Shay Culligan

ISBN: 978-1-952326-74-5

Kelsay Books
502 South 1040 East, A-119
American Fork, Utah, 84003

To us

Acknowledgments

All of the poems contained in this volume first saw the light of day on trains, buses, trams, ferries, and subway systems across China's concrete expanse.

Half of them appeared in a variety of online and print outlets:

The Cabinet of Heed: "Medea"

Poetry Breakfast: "Persephone"

Nine Muses Poetry: "Polyphemus"

Down in the Dirt Magazine: "Cassandra," "Romulus," "Phaethon," "Andromeda"

Pure Slush: "Alexander"

Artis Natura: "Chloris"

Scarlet Leaf Review: "Arria," "Xerxes"

Amethyst Review: "Iphigenia," "Minotaur"

Bluepepper: "Pandora"

None would have come to be written and read without those countless individuals in public transport and publishing on whose indispensable—if sometimes unwitting—contribution I depend.

Contents

Medea

harness a raging fire
arrest a torrent in its rush
bleed the heart of a rock
you can

the gore and the dross
left in your wake
singe as they swell
in the only space there is

flesh blood skin bone
anointed and enhanced
proliferate
beyond the wine-dark sea

you may wish to move on
new life awaiting you
in faraway climes
but no.

Persephone

Has she been trapped
too deep
in darkness by desire
away from the sky she grew up with

Has she been a captive
of the underworld
for too long
fueled by its attractive forces

Has she been held
under too enthralling a spell
to renounce the powers
of making things wither

Is it now too late for her
to emerge out into the light
fresh-faced and innocent of heart
and believe everything is going to be fine

Polyphemus

It might have been a faint distant echo
of worlds
lost
or saved
on islands adrift amid the wine-dark sea

So they came
with their new words
different views and scents
looking back toward foreign lands
on their ships like nothing ever seen before

With the strength young muscles muster
and the cunning of new ideas
they snuck in
they asked and answered
and burned old eyes out for their stories

Being the shape
of all things to come
they were well within their rights
the ways of the ones before had to yield
redeemed by their sacrifice to the dead-end new

Cassandra

She was first
to behold it
from the spires

they dragged Her name
disgraced
tarred and feathered
through the fora

Her cries warned
the wretched
of their common woe

they nailed Her memory
high up
across
the boards

heart aflame
She yelled
portents of calamity

they mobbed Her
shamed Her
for evil speech
empty words

She took an axe
and a torch
to save them

they ambushed Her
stripped Her
abandoned Her
and reveled till the end

She might as well
have been wrong
and died unaware
not
alone

Charybdis

Shore by shore
coast to coast
maps engulfed
on a nightly basis
ever inland

Boundaries revealed
to have been constructs
inhibitions
we had to feel we needed

Re-claimed lands taken back
the presumptuous prefix
in sharp relief

Depressions all filled in
with the elemental swill
of busyness on the way out

The vertical
giving in to the horizontal
along oh along
a gentle unforgiving slope

Among it all
the three of them
two of legacy
one of promise
neither to be kept

Caught in between
mouths and bellies too small
to swallow any of it
no matter how thirsty
or hungry or scared

Romulus

Suckled
fostered
nurtured
sheltered
moisturized
wiped and burped
you moved on.

Warmth she gave
exploited as fuel
nutrition she shared
drained for your fields
shade she offered
replaced with alternatives
to power you up.

Making the gestures
when expected to
saying the words
when you should
nodding along
you do you
and have dominion.

While abandoned
used and abused
exploited
polluted
mined
fracked
she is changing.

Telemachus

Move on
He's not coming
with words of wisdom
wrinkles in the corners of his eyes
callused hands
to your aid

He knows
or doesn't
or doesn't mind
either way
he wants to live out his life
while you need to save yours

It was his decision
his purpose
his pride, too
that you would be left behind
an afterthought
in all but name

If he did come
what would he do
what would he made you do
to reassert himself
and what good would that do
to anyone

His maps outdated
routes misguided
priorities anchored in the past
all he could do is slow you down
when every moment matters
and every life

Dido

Now wasn't that clever
To take so much so cheap
Based on a technicality

A corner of my lips
Raised ever so slightly
I made things happen

Carving defiant words
I walked on
Eyes hard ahead

Hands gripped and gripping
I'd rather see all burn
Than let go

Caught up with at last
Encircled and encompassed
I climbed my pyre

What followed was me
Lips, eyes, and hands
In a different tongue

Taking still more
They made things happen
As salt ate through my bones

Alexander

A stirring story under his pillow
he warred on distant lands
to rule the ends of the world

Drunk on his own name
he scorched restless roads
through silence and shade

Looking up to his gods
he fantasized of immortality
earthly bounds be damned

Not stopped by his people
he would have sunk the sun itself
in the outer seas

Not undone by his flaws
he would have drenched the dead
in the tears of survivors

Not ended by his fever
he would have drowned multitudes
in their own blood

And then died anyway.

Circe

Consumption
just used to mean
your body wasting away
now it means the world

It's all convenient
to use
to swallow
to let it run through your veins

Potions and poisons
now dyes and drugs
catchy phrases and funny pics
flavor enhancers

Tools of your own tools
you're hooked
wanting out
while stuffing on feed

Winds trapped in your sails
trees felled for your masts
waves thick with your filth
the hazy edge closing in

Confident, you smile.

Semiramis

Isn't it nice
to tell ourselves
we can enjoy the view
safe in the knowledge
it's built to last

Orderly fields of grass
surrounding

Neat rows of trees
flanking

Long lines of flowerbeds
blockading

Camouflaged
in blameless ambush

Wild strength
trimmed
creative power
pruned
networks and systems
dismembered
as long as we're armed
with sharp metal
fresh concrete
confidence of numbers

Garden cities
and concrete ones
will overgrow
overwhelm
and the myth long since gone
it won't be them hanging

Enthroned in the trap
we tune the tripwire

Phaethon

Greatly he dared

Reaching up high
for more than he could handle
staring far ahead
towards the all too bright
against better judgement
in spite of warnings
pushed by unsuitable instincts
pulled by irrelevant impulses
imagining himself to know
to be in control
to have a global view
to foresee consequences
to equal gods

More greatly he failed

Andromeda

Wingless
Finless
You have nowhere else to go

Tied down in two dimensions
Immobilized by your past
You await

You already see it rising
Inch by inch
But you are good at looking away

No godlike superhero
Is about to rescue you
And make it all go away

Once it's here
You will have to face it
For what it is

And you will embrace it
As it ends you
Because it's your own

Antaeus

Better traction
on asphalt surfaces
taller structures
over concrete foundations
faster transport
through combusted air
farther access
with synthetic polymers

Don't you have it all
and more
figured out

Habituated to progress
instinctively expansive
hungry for power
pushing the limits
reaching high up
poisoning the source
self-serving by definition
over-confident to the core

Didn't you lose touch
just before being challenged
for once

Hypatia

Who dreams to be
the symbol of a vanished world
twisted and tweaked
to fit the story

There used to be
more
that was abandoned
in the upheavals of time

Hard-worn understanding
ideas worth sharing
facts and figures
that didn't fit the later minds

Preserving what's left
is a full-time job
that pays little
and costs everything

Too many
who'd rather not know
stand in stubborn confidence
on the eroding shore

Amassing all there is
won't guarantee anything
the forgetting happened before
after all

Epimetheus

You shouldn't have stolen it
now look at them

inflamed by its heat
that feeds on itself
they blaze through the world

powered by its glow
they incandesce the dark
and irradiate the shade

consumed by its rage
they burn the dead and the unborn
to fuel the living

now what
brother?

Chloris

They say
you used to turn gods and humans
into flowers.

There must have been
many of them then.

We remember the meadows
the woods
the rolling plains
or perhaps we could.

They're here
everywhere
in the past we exploit
for our present purposes.

But we don't
a captive flowerbed
trimmed and encircled
being our nature of choice.

And why would we
walking
working
living as we do
on the paved-over mass grave
of them all.

Scylla

If only someone else could
Be blamed a jealous
Rival perhaps that
Poured poisonous potion into
Your bath

If only someone else was
To blame for taking
Away your beauty in
A vicious plot you had
Nothing to do with

If only it could be blamed
On someone else that innocent
As you were you became a
Victim deserving
Of pity and forgiveness

But it was you
In your bone and blood
Who made the choices
Ignored the realities
And turned into the monster

Astyanax

It's only a question of time
no matter our guiding words
our loving touch
our money.

It won't be long
the future is going to catch up
make you pay
for the legacy we're leaving.

It'll be over soon
because we took what's yours
the green and the blue
leaving sludge and smoke.

It's all just one step away
over the edge
perhaps it's better
if you go now.

Arria

Shrouded in leaves and bark
its branches on the ground
made her look up

Against the concrete wall
she remembered
it stood
still

The lunch break all but over
the metal would be back soon
to finish the job

She touched what was left
raised her hand to her hair
and with a vision of herself
growing up as it grew tall
she pulled at a strand
just big enough
winced
groaned
and held it up high

'It doesn't hurt,' she said
as passers-by walked on

Cincinnatus

No
he didn't
keep his word

The ploughing
and the tilling
was not to do harm

The planting
and the harvesting
was not to take root

He ought to have
returned home
and let it be

Trees unfelled
rivers undammed
seasons unchanged

His honor unblemished
status unchallenged
livelihood unquestioned

But he stayed

Iphigenia

The sacrifices I've made
the offerings and the victims
have all been in her name

The wealth I create
by the hard work I do
        exploiting air and water
        stimulating demand
        processing foodstuffs
        utilizing other life forms
        moving money around
        providing distractions
        turning earth into fire
ensures I have the means
to be a good parent

She will surely appreciate
the shiny altar built for her
as she goes on alone

Minotaur

They say you were lurking
in the shadows
waiting for the right time
to strike.

I say you were hiding
away from prying eyes
hoping
to be left alone.

You say you were
raw material
for others
to make their name.

He says your life
and your death
gave him
his immortal fame.

She says nothing
with a frown
resting her head
on his shoulder.

We say you were a hybrid
a monster
an abomination
a god.

Who says you were a species?

Pollux

This was never fair
caught off guard
blindsided
wronged
he would have to go
and you wouldn't

Perfect form
mirror image
unspoken assumption
casting a shadow
onto the only reality
that had to be him

It was always one-way
dead-end
landmined
with a mirage of you
leading him on
for the benefit of others

Can't blame you
you don't exist
he does
but he didn't have to
and given what's coming
he shouldn't

Artemis

tastes bitter to say this
now that they are the ones
who defend

what little is left

marginal land
is all they've got
though once they roamed free

in the garden

the giving nature
nurtured their genes
ideas and entitlements

they took root and branch

they know their land
and respect it
once they transformed it

one generation after next

rituals and traditions
quaint and harmless to your eyes
did their odd job long ago

now it all seems finely tuned

the wisdom they share
is two-faced
however guilty you feel

their demise all but complete

the blood-won harmony
they bequeathed to all
breaks and fills your heart

there was never a better way

if you're not too invested
to see
you might just make it

through

Narcissus

With all you could see
why would you only
see yourself

Is this inward gaze
the best use
of your attention

All the others
and elsewheres
aren't worth a look

Your focus
firm and fixed
can you notice all there is

Isn't your intent stare
not much better
than shutting your eyes

Deep down
in your tunnel vision
are you aware you're vanishing

The pool filling up with your filth
how can you be sure
you know your face

Xerxes

Microplastics and CO_2
Desertification and smog
Landfills and algal blooms
Flooding and deforestation
Mudslides and sand mining
Fracking and feedback loops
Fertilizer runoff and oil spills
Coral bleaching and droughts
Melting glaciers and tar sands
Heat waves and degraded soils
Toxic waste and failing harvests
Hurricanes and depleted aquifers
Biodiversity loss and oil pipelines
Light pollution and rising sea levels
Ocean acidification and tipping points
Albedo effect and collapsing fish stocks
Saltwater intrusion and extinction events
Thawing permafrost and radiative forcing
Methane clathrates and shrinking ice caps
Resource depletion and urban heat islands
Ecocide and anthropogenic climate change
Power structures, short-termism, and greed
This is why I'm weeping

Pandora

and now they're out
for good
released and at large
not going back underground
not leaving either
red-hot and self-sustained

levers and engines
generic condemnations
personal sacrifices
signatures and ratifications
won't slow the winds
calm the seas

all that's left with us
is false
and blind
tucking us in
with a reassuring smile
while what we need is courage

About the Author

Dawid Juraszek is a bilingual author and educator based in China and an external PhD candidate at Maastricht University working on cognitive ecocriticism. A published novelist in his native Poland, his poetry, fiction, and non-fiction have appeared in multiple outlets in the United States, Great Britain, Australia, Canada, and Ireland.

~

Visit https://amazon.com/author/dawidjuraszek